HWA-RANG
and
CHUNG-MU

WARNING

This book is presented only as a means of preserving a unique aspect of the heritage of the martial arts. Neither Ohara Publications nor the author makes any representation, warranty or guarantee that the techniques described in this book will be safe or effective in any self-defense situation or otherwise. You may be injured if you apply or train in the techniques of self-defense illustrated in this book, and neither Ohara Publications nor the author is responsible for any such injury that may result. It is essential that you consult a physician regarding whether or not to attempt any technique described in this book. Specific self-defense responses illustrated in this book may not be justified in any particular situation in view of all of the circumstances or under the applicable federal, state or local law. Neither Ohara Publications nor the author makes any representation or warranty regarding the legality or appropriateness of any technique mentioned in this book.

HWA-RANG and CHUNG-MU
OF TAE KWON DO HYUNG

By JHOON RHEE

Hwa-Rang and Chung-Mu are two of the hyungs required
by the International Tae Kwon Do Federation.

OHARA 🔟 PUBLICATIONS, INCORPORATED
SANTA CLARITA, CALIFORNIA

I would like to express my sincere appreciation to my photographers,
Mr. Jimmy Rudd
And
Mr. Ku Kyung Chung

© Ohara Publications, Incorporated 1971
Printed in the United States of America
Library of Congress Catalog Card Number: 77-163382

Eighteenth printing 2001

ISBN 0-89750-004-0

PREFACE

Although introduced only recently in the western world, the art of Tae Kwon Do has become increasingly popular in all countries and with all age groups. Originally conceived in Korea as a measure of unarmed self-defense, Tae Kwon Do has blossomed into an art that is now practiced all over the world.

This book has been written with several purposes in mind. First of all, it is intended to develop a greater appreciation and understanding of Tae Kwon Do, which would contribute toward the growth of this ancient martial art. Since it includes explicit instructions and detailed guidance on all aspects of the art, it will serve as a basic text for beginners. To the intermediate students, this text provides a firm foundation for the more complicated patterns and advanced techniques which follow. It also serves as an authoritative reference on all phases of Tae Kwon Do training for the instructors.

HWA-RANG and CHUNG-MU is the fifth in a series of five volumes covering nine of the major hyungs of Tae Kwon Do. The first book deals with the Chon-Ji hyung required at the white belt level. The second book deals with Tan-Gun and To-San which are required at the gold belt level. The third book deals with Won-Hyo and Yul-Kok which are required for the green belt level. The fourth book deals with Chung-Gun and Toi-Gye which are required at the blue belt level. This is the final book in a series of five dealing with the hyungs required in order to obtain the black belt.

It is my most sincere wish that this book will embody the true essence of Tae Kwon Do—the discipline and humility which arise from one's dedication to the art. Without such spirit, the student's training is incomplete; with it, he becomes master of himself. For both the physical and spiritual fulfillment of Tae Kwon Do, then, this book is humbly dedicated.

Jhoon Rhee

SENATOR MILTON R. YOUNG
President — U.S. Tae Kwon Do Association

AUTHOR JHOON RHEE

CONTENTS

WHAT IS TAE KWON DO?

Tae Kwon Do is a Korean martial art which has been developed through centuries of Eastern civilization. Today Tae Kwon Do has evolved into not only the most effective method of weaponless self-defense but an intricate art, an exciting sport and a trenchant method of maintaining physical fitness.

Many think that breaking boards and bricks is what Tae Kwon Do consists of, but this is an entirely mistaken concept. Demonstrations displaying such feats merely show the power and speed the human body is capable of utilizing through Tae Kwon Do training.

Tremendous skill and control are required in Tae Kwon Do. While blocking, kicking and punching techniques all contribute to making Tae Kwon Do one of the most exciting and competitive sports, its challenge lies in the adept use of techniques without having any actual body contact. Complete control over punching and kicking movements is paramount in stopping just centimeters short of the opponent.

Through the coordination of control, balance and technique in the performance of hyungs (patterns), Tae Kwon Do is regarded as a beautiful and highly skilled martial art. It is also one of the most all-around methods of physical fitness since it utilizes every single muscle of the body and is considered the ultimate in unarmed self-defense. In Korea, the Presidential Protective Forces are all trained in Tae Kwon Do and several other countries are adopting it into the training programs of their protective forces as well.

WHAT ARE HYUNGS?

One of the more important aspects of Tae Kwon Do training is learning Tae Kwon Do hyungs, a set series of attacking and defensive movements which follow a logical, predetermined sequence. Although each hyung comprises different movements or techniques, there are certain basic elements common to all:

1) Each hyung begins and ends from the same point.
2) All movements are performed at speeds and rhythms conforming to those established by the hyungs being performed.
3) All movements must be performed with rapid facing and correct posture.

Each hyung in itself is of immense value in the physical and mental development of the student since it serves many purposes. As a means of physical conditioning, it develops the student's balance, muscle coordination and endurance which ultimately leads to increased self-discipline.

Hyungs also give the student the opportunity to practice the ideal blocking and attacking movements against an imaginary opponent. Just as the student in school learns to print, so his handwriting is a departure from the ideal and becomes a mark of his personal style. The same may be said for Tae Kwon Do. A student's sparring or fighting style becomes his adaptation of the principles he has acquired from hyungs. The hyungs, then, are the student's line between Tae Kwon Do training and actual fighting.

Finally, hyungs are a graphic demonstration of the art of Tae Kwon Do that is a mark of the level of development the student has acquired. As a student progresses he undertakes more complex hyungs. They are designed to challenge and make him call upon his resources and all that he has learned in order to perform the new movements and increase his scope of discipline and development.

Tae Kwon Do hyungs have been developed and perfected throughout the centuries by the outstanding teachers of the art. Each hyung consists of the most logical movements of blocking, punching, striking or kicking possible within that sequence of movements. A student should not attempt to take on a new hyung until he has perfected the hyungs he is required to learn at his level of achievement. Before advancing to another hyung it is customary for a student to perform the one he is presently learning at least 300 times.

WITH WHAT HYUNG DOES EACH RANK TRAIN?

HYUNG	RANK (Class)	COLOR BELT	AMOUNT PERFORMED
Chon-Ji	10th & 9th	White	At Least 300 Times
Tan-Gun	8th	Gold	At Least 300 Times
To-San	7th	Gold	At Least 300 Times
Won-Hyo	6th	Green	At Least 300 Times
Yul-Kok	5th	Green	At Least 300 Times
Chung-Gun	4th	Blue	At Least 300 Times
Toi-Gye	3rd	Blue	At Least 300 Times
Hwa-Rang	2nd	Brown	At Least 300 Times
Chung-Mu	1st	Brown	At Least 300 Times

REQUIREMENTS FOR 1ST DEGREE BLACK BELT

1. Right attitude and good character.

2. Mastery of the aforementioned nine patterns.

3. Capability of breaking three, one-inch pine boards with the following techniques:

   a. straight punch

   b. knife-hand strike

   c. front or roundhouse kick

   d. side snap kick

4. Good free-sparring ability coupled with well-controlled techniques.

5. Ability and willingness to teach the tenets of Tae Kwon Do to others.

HWA-RANG HYUNG

Hwa-Rang is named after the Hwa-Rang youth group which originated in the Silla Dynasty about 1,350 years ago and became the actual driving force for the unification of the three Kingdoms of Korea.

DIAGRAM

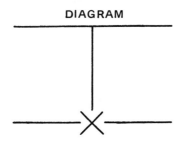

HWA-RANG
AT A GLANCE

READY

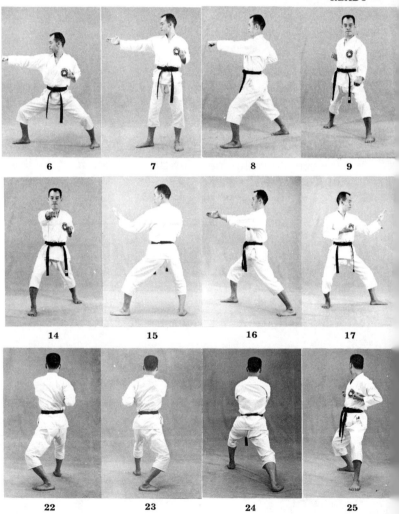

6	7	8	9
14	15	16	17
22	23	24	25

18

1   2   3   4   5

10   11   12A   12B   13

18   19A   19B   20   21

26   27   28   29   END

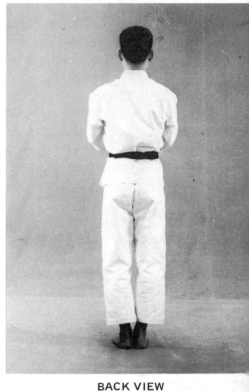

SIDE VIEW

BACK VIEW

OTHER VIEW

STEP DIAGRAM

CHUNBI SOGI

(Ready Stance)

Assume a closed ready stance "C" with hands crossed—left covering right at low hip level.

NOTE: All pivotal turns indicated in degrees, either clockwise or counterclockwise, refer to the directional turn of the face. Star symbols (★) indicate KIHAP (yelling).

FRONT VIEW

TOP VIEW

APPLICATION

BEGINNING FRONT VIEW

INTERMEDIATE FRONT VIEW

OTHER VIEW

STEP DIAGRAM

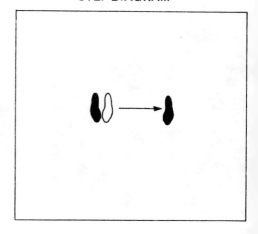

1. CHUNGDAN CHANGKWON MARKI

(Middle Palm Heel Block)

Step out to the left with the left foot, assuming a riding stance as you execute a middle pushing block with left palm fist.*

FINAL FRONT VIEW

TOP VIEW

APPLICATION

OTHER VIEW

STEP DIAGRAM

2. CHUNGDAN KIMA SOGI CHIRUGI
(Middle Riding Stance Punch)

Execute a middle punch with the right fist.

FINAL FRONT VIEW

TOP VIEW	APPLICATION

OTHER VIEW

STEP DIAGRAM

 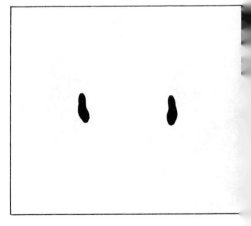

3. CHUNGDAN
KIMA SOGI CHIRUGI
(Middle Riding Stance Punch)

Execute a middle punch with the left fist.

FINAL FRONT VIEW

TOP VIEW

APPLICATION

BEGINNING FRONT VIEW

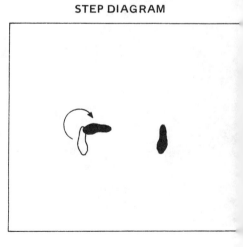

INTERMEDIATE FRONT VIEW

OTHER VIEW

STEP DIAGRAM

4. SANG PALMOK MARKI

(Twin Forearm Block)

Pull the right foot inward as you pivot on the left foot 90 degrees clockwise, assuming a left back stance as you execute a twin forearm block.

FINAL FRONT VIEW

TOP VIEW

APPLICATION

BEGINNING FRONT VIEW　　　　**INTERMEDIATE FRONT VIEW**

OTHER VIEW　　　　**STEP DIAGRAM**

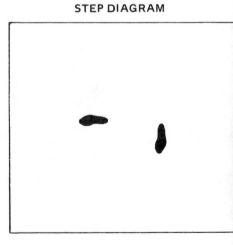

5. CHUNGDAN PALMOK ANURO MARKI
(Middle Forearm Inward Block)

Execute a middle inward block with the left forearm as you pull the right fist in front of the left shoulder.

FINAL FRONT VIEW

TOP VIEW

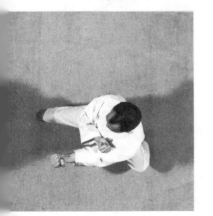

APPLICATION

BEGINNING FRONT VIEW   **INTERMEDIATE FRONT VIEW**

OTHER VIEW   **STEP DIAGRAM**

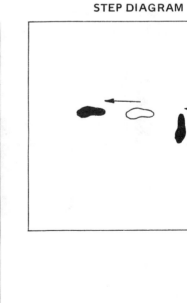

6. CHUNGDAN YOP CHIRUGI

(Middle Side Punch)

Slide both feet forward, assuming a right fixed stance as you execute a middle side punch with the right fist.

FINAL FRONT VIEW

TOP VIEW

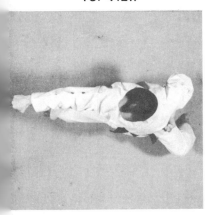

APPLICATION

33

BEGINNING FRONT VIEW   **INTERMEDIATE FRONT VIEW**

OTHER VIEW   **STEP DIAGRAM**

 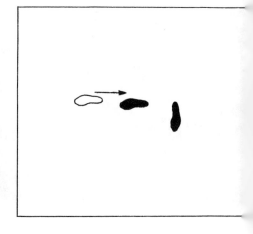

7. SUDO NAERYO TAERIGI
(Knife-Hand Downward Strike)

Pull the right foot inward until it is about a foot's length away from the left foot, as you execute a downward strike with the right knife-hand.

FINAL FRONT VIEW

TOP VIEW

APPLICATION

35

BEGINNING FRONT VIEW

INTERMEDIATE FRONT VIEW

OTHER VIEW

STEP DIAGRAM

36

8. CHUNGDAN CHIRUGI
(Middle Punch)

Take a straight step with the left foot, assuming a left front stance as you execute a middle punch with the left fist.

FINAL FRONT VIEW

TOP VIEW	APPLICATION

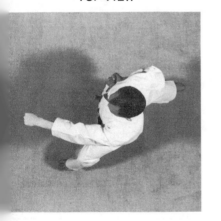

BEGINNING FRONT VIEW

INTERMEDIATE FRONT VIEW

OTHER VIEW

STEP DIAGRAM

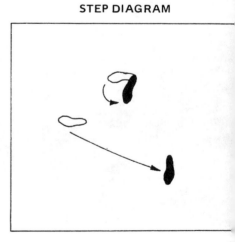

9. HARDAN PALMOK MARKI

(Low Forearm Block)

Pivot on the right foot 90 degrees counterclockwise, assuming a left front stance as you execute a low block with the left forearm.

FINAL FRONT VIEW

TOP VIEW

APPLICATION

BEGINNING FRONT VIEW

INTERMEDIATE FRONT VIEW

OTHER VIEW

STEP DIAGRAM

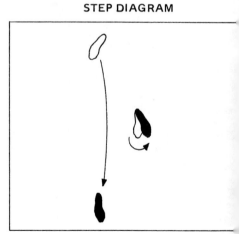

10. CHUNGDAN CHIRUGI

(Middle Punch)

Take a straight step with the right foot, assuming a right front stance as you execute a middle punch with the right fist.

FINAL FRONT VIEW

TOP VIEW

APPLICATION

BEGINNING FRONT VIEW

INTERMEDIATE FRONT VIEW

OTHER VIEW

STEP DIAGRAM

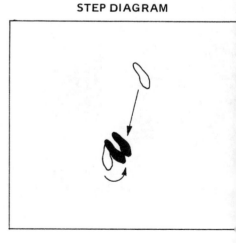

42

11. YOP CHAGI CHUNBI SOGI
(Side Kick Ready Stance)

Bring the left foot alongside the right foot, assuming a side kick ready stance as you cover the right fist with the left palm.

FINAL FRONT VIEW

TOP VIEW

APPLICATION

BEGINNING FRONT VIEW

INTERMEDIATE FRONT VIEW

OTHER VIEW

STEP DIAGRAMS

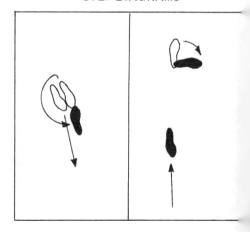

12. CHUNGDAN YOP CHAGI

(Middle Side Thrust Kick)

Pull both hands inward as you execute a middle side thrust kick with the right foot. Lower the kicking foot, assuming a left back stance as you execute a middle side strike with the right knife-hand.

FINAL FRONT VIEW

TOP VIEW

APPLICATION

BEGINNING FRONT VIEW

INTERMEDIATE FRONT VIEW

OTHER VIEW

STEP DIAGRAM

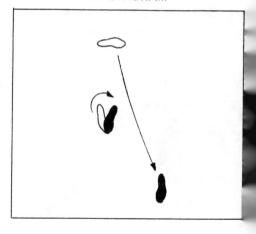

13.CHUNGDAN CHIRUGI

(Middle Punch)

Take a straight step with the left foot, assuming a left front stance as you execute a middle punch with the left fist.

FINAL FRONT VIEW

TOP VIEW

APPLICATION

47

BEGINNING FRONT VIEW

OTHER VIEW

INTERMEDIATE FRONT VIEW

STEP DIAGRAM

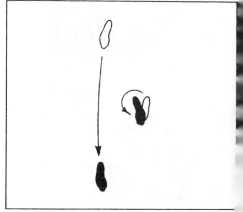

14. CHUNGDAN CHIRUGI
(Middle Punch)

Take a straight step with the right foot, assuming a right front stance as you execute a middle punch with the right fist. ★

FINAL FRONT VIEW

TOP VIEW

APPLICATION

BEGINNING FRONT VIEW

INTERMEDIATE FRONT VIEW

OTHER VIEW

STEP DIAGRAM

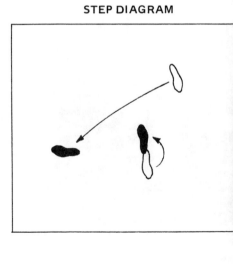

50

15. CHUNGDAN SUDO MARKI
(Middle Knife-Hand Block)

Pivot on the right foot 270 degrees counterclockwise, assuming a right back stance as you execute a middle block with the left knife-hand.

FINAL FRONT VIEW

TOP VIEW

APPLICATION

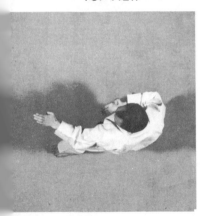

BEGINNING FRONT VIEW

INTERMEDIATE FRONT VIEW

OTHER VIEW

STEP DIAGRAM

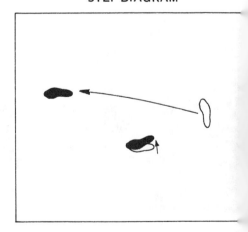

16. CHUNGDAN KWANSU
(Middle Spear-Finger)

Take a straight step with the right foot, assuming a right front stance as you execute a vertical spear-finger thrust with the right hand.

FINAL FRONT VIEW

TOP VIEW

APPLICATION

BEGINNING FRONT VIEW

INTERMEDIATE FRONT VIEW

OTHER VIEW

STEP DIAGRAM

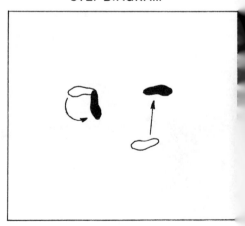

17. CHUNGDAN SUDO MARKI
(Middle Knife-Hand Block)

Pivot on the right foot 180 degrees counterclockwise, assuming a right back stance as you execute a middle block with the left knife-hand.

FINAL FRONT VIEW

TOP VIEW

APPLICATION

BEGINNING FRONT VIEW

INTERMEDIATE FRONT VIEW

OTHER VIEW

STEP DIAGRAM

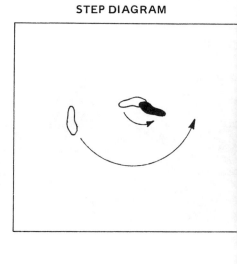

18. SANGDAN TOLYO CHAGI
(High Roundhouse Kick)

Execute a high roundhouse kick with the right foot, then step straight down with the kicking foot.

FINAL FRONT VIEW

TOP VIEW   **APPLICATION**

BEGINNING FRONT VIEW

INTERMEDIATE FRONT VIEW

TOP VIEW

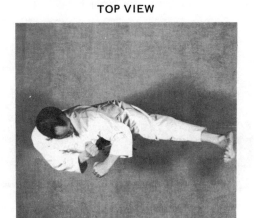

STEP DIAGRAM

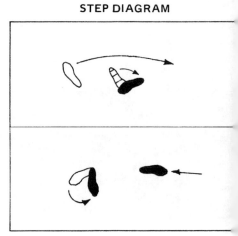

19. SANGDAN TOLYO CHAGI

(High Roundhouse Kick)

Execute a high roundhouse kick with the left foot, then step straight down with the kicking foot, assuming a right back stance as you execute a middle block with the left knife-hand.

FINAL FRONT VIEW

APPLICATION

APPLICATION

BEGINNING FRONT VIEW

INTERMEDIATE FRONT VIEW

OTHER VIEW

STEP DIAGRAM

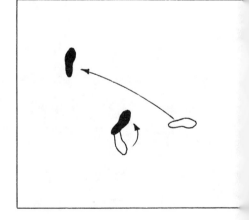

FINAL FRONT VIEW

20. HARDAN PALMOK MARKI
(Low Forearm Block)

Pivot on the right foot 90 degrees counterclockwise, assuming a left front stance as you execute a low block with the left forearm.

TOP VIEW

APPLICATION

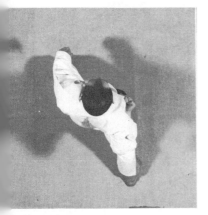

BEGINNING FRONT VIEW

INTERMEDIATE FRONT VIEW

OTHER VIEW

STEP DIAGRAM

21. CHUNGDAN FUGUL PANDAE CHIRUGI
(Middle Back Stance Reverse Punch)

Pull the left foot inward, assuming a right back stance as you execute a middle reverse punch with the right fist.

FINAL FRONT VIEW

TOP VIEW

APPLICATION

BEGINNING FRONT VIEW

INTERMEDIATE FRONT VIEW

OTHER VIEW

STEP DIAGRAM

22. CHUNGDAN FUGUL PANDAE CHIRUGI

(Middle Back Stance Reverse Punch)

Take a straight step with the right foot, assuming a left back stance as you execute a middle reverse punch with the left fist.

FINAL FRONT VIEW

TOP VIEW

APPLICATION

BEGINNING FRONT VIEW   **INTERMEDIATE FRONT VIEW**

OTHER VIEW   **STEP DIAGRAM**

23. CHUNGDAN FUGUL PANDAE CHIRUGI

(Middle Back Stance Reverse Punch)

Take a straight step with the left foot, assuming a right back stance as you execute a middle reverse punch with the right fist.

FINAL FRONT VIEW

TOP VIEW

APPLICATION

BEGINNING FRONT VIEW

INTERMEDIATE FRONT VIEW

OTHER VIEW

STEP DIAGRAM

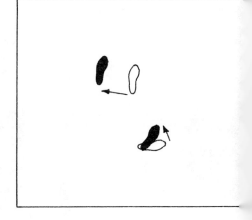

24. KYOCHA JOOMOK NAERYO MARKI
(X Fist Down Block)

Slide the left foot forward, assuming a left front stance as you execute a low X fist down block.

FINAL FRONT VIEW

TOP VIEW	APPLICATION

BEGINNING FRONT VIEW

INTERMEDIATE FRONT VIEW

OTHER VIEW

STEP DIAGRAM

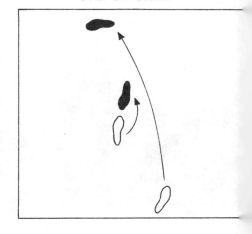

FINAL FRONT VIEW

25. CHUNGDAN PALKUMCHI TAERIGI
(Middle Elbow Strike)

Pivot on the left foot 180 degrees counterclockwise and slide, assuming a right back stance as you execute a middle elbow strike with the right elbow.

TOP VIEW

APPLICATION

BEGINNING FRONT VIEW

INTERMEDIATE FRONT VIEW

OTHER VIEW

STEP DIAGRAM

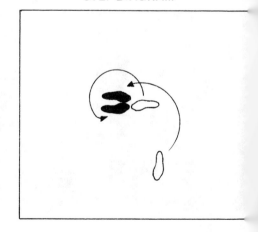

26. SANG HARDAN MARKI
(High-Low Closed Stance Block)

Bring the left foot alongside the right foot as you pivot on the right foot 90 degrees counterclockwise, assuming a closed stance. Execute a high-low block with both forearms.

FINAL FRONT VIEW

TOP VIEW

APPLICATION

BEGINNING FRONT VIEW

INTERMEDIATE FRONT VIEW

OTHER VIEW

STEP DIAGRAM

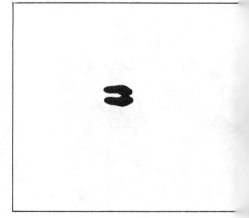

27. SANG HARDAN MARKI

(High-Low Closed Stance Block)

Reverse the position of the arms, executing a high-low block with both forearms.

FINAL FRONT VIEW

TOP VIEW

APPLICATION

BEGINNING FRONT VIEW

INTERMEDIATE FRONT VIEW

OTHER VIEW

STEP DIAGRAM

28. CHUNGDAN SUDO MARKI

(Middle Knife-Hand Block)

Take a straight step with the left foot, assuming a right back stance as you execute a middle block with the left knife-hand.

FINAL FRONT VIEW

TOP VIEW

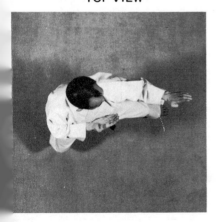

APPLICATION

BEGINNING FRONT VIEW

INTERMEDIATE FRONT VIEW

OTHER VIEW

STEP DIAGRAM

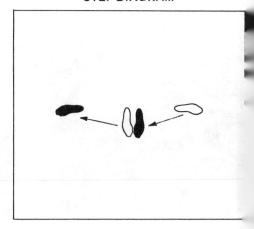

29. CHUNGDAN SUDO MARKI

(Middle Knife-Hand Block)

Bring the left foot alongside the right foot, then step out with the right foot, assuming a left back stance as you execute a middle block with the right knife-hand. ★

FINAL FRONT VIEW

TOP VIEW

APPLICATION

SIDE VIEW

BACK VIEW

OTHER VIEW

STEP DIAGRAM

80

GOMAN
(End)

Bring the right foot alongside the left foot, assuming a closed ready stance "C" with hands crossed—left covering right at low hip level.

FRONT VIEW

TOP VIEW

APPLICATION

CHUNG-MU HYUNG

Chung-Mu was the given name of the great Admiral Yi Sun-Sin of the Yi Dynasty who was reputed to have invented the first armoured battleship—the precursor of the present-day submarine—in 1592 A.D. The left-hand attack ending this pattern symbolizes his regrettable death in battle before he had a chance to show his complete loyalty to the King.

DIAGRAM

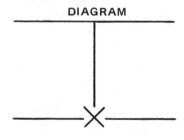

CHUNG-MU AT A GLANCE

READY 1 2

8 9A 9B 10

16 17 18 19A

24A 24B 25 26

SIDE VIEW

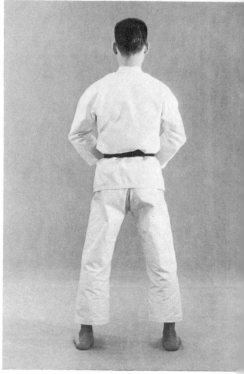

BACK VIEW

OTHER VIEW

STEP DIAGRAM

CHUNBI SOGI

(Ready Stance)

Assume a parallel ready stance.

NOTE: All pivotal turns indicated in degrees, either clockwise or counter-clockwise, refer to the directional turn of the face. Star symbols (★) indicate KIHAP (yelling).

FRONT VIEW

TOP VIEW

APPLICATION

BEGINNING FRONT VIEW

INTERMEDIATE FRONT VIEW

OTHER VIEW

STEP DIAGRAM

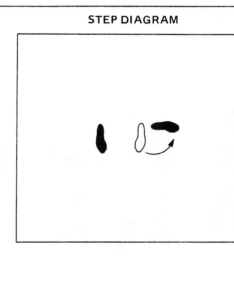

88

1. SANG
SUDO MARKI
(Twin Knife-Hand Block)

Pivot on the right foot 90 degrees counterclockwise, assuming a right back stance as you execute a twin knife-hand block. ★

TOP VIEW

APPLICATION

BEGINNING FRONT VIEW

INTERMEDIATE FRONT VIEW

OTHER VIEW

STEP DIAGRAM

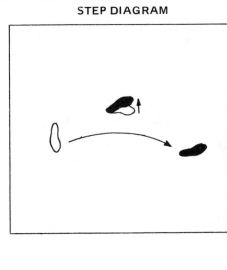

2. SANGDAN SUDO ANURO TAERIGI

(High Inward Knife-Hand Strike)

Take a straight step with the right foot, assuming a right front stance as you execute a high inward strike with the right knife-hand and bring the left knife-hand in front of the forehead.

FINAL FRONT VIEW

TOP VIEW

APPLICATION

BEGINNING FRONT VIEW

INTERMEDIATE FRONT VIEW

OTHER VIEW

STEP DIAGRAM

3. CHUNGDAN SUDO MARKI

(Middle Knife-Hand Block)

Pivot on the left foot 180 degrees clockwise, assuming a left back stance as you execute a middle guarding block with the right knife-hand.

FINAL FRONT VIEW

TOP VIEW	APPLICATION

BEGINNING FRONT VIEW | **INTERMEDIATE FRONT VIEW**

OTHER VIEW | **STEP DIAGRAM**

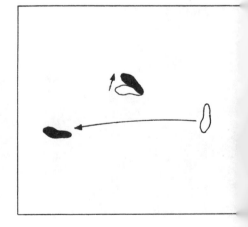

FINAL FRONT VIEW

4. SANGDAN KWANSU

(High Spear-Finger)

Take a straight step with the left foot, assuming a left front stance as you execute a high thrust with the left spear-hand.

TOP VIEW

APPLICATION

BEGINNING FRONT VIEW   **INTERMEDIATE FRONT VIEW**

OTHER VIEW   **STEP DIAGRAM**

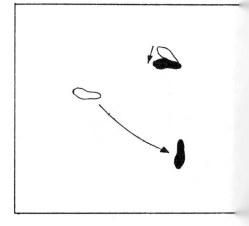

FINAL FRONT VIEW

5. CHUNGDAN SUDO MARKI
(Middle Knife-Hand Block)

Pivot on the right foot 90 degrees counterclockwise, assuming a right back stance as you execute a middle guarding block with the left knife-hand.

TOP VIEW	APPLICATION

BEGINNING FRONT VIEW

INTERMEDIATE FRONT VIEW

OTHER VIEW

STEP DIAGRAM

FINAL FRONT VIEW

6. YOP CHAGI CHUNBI SOGI
(Side Kick Ready Stance)

Bring the right fist to the top of the left fist as you bring your right foot to your left foot.

TOP VIEW

APPLICATION

BEGINNING FRONT VIEW

INTERMEDIATE FRONT VIEW

OTHER VIEW

STEP DIAGRAM

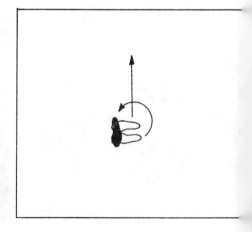

100

FINAL FRONT VIEW

7. CHUNGDAN YOP CHAGI
(Middle Side Thrust Kick)

Execute a middle side thrusting kick with the right foot.

TOP VIEW	APPLICATION

BEGINNING FRONT VIEW

INTERMEDIATE FRONT VIEW

OTHER VIEW

STEP DIAGRAM

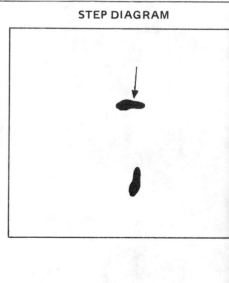

102

8. CHUNGDAN SUDO MARKI

(Middle Knife-Hand Block)

Lower the right foot, assuming a right back stance as you execute a middle guarding block with the left knife-hand.

FINAL FRONT VIEW

TOP VIEW

APPLICATION

BEGINNING FRONT VIEW

INTERMEDIATE FRONT VIEW

TOP VIEW

STEP DIAGRAM

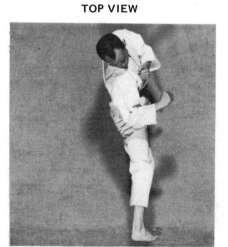

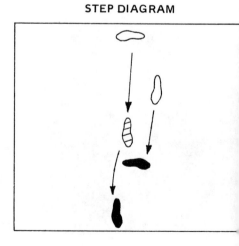

9. TUIYO YOP CHAGI
(Jump Side Kick)

Step forward with the right foot, then execute a jump side kick with the right foot in a double motion. Land in a left back stance as you execute a middle guarding block with the right knife-hand.★

FINAL FRONT VIEW

APPLICATIONS

BEGINNING FRONT VIEW

INTERMEDIATE FRONT VIEW

OTHER VIEW

STEP DIAGRAM

10. HARDAN PALMOK MARKI

(Low Forearm Block)

Pivot on the right foot 270 degrees counterclockwise, assuming a right back stance as you execute a low block with the left forearm.

FINAL FRONT VIEW

TOP VIEW

APPLICATION

BEGINNING FRONT VIEW

INTERMEDIATE FRONT VIEW

OTHER VIEW

STEP DIAGRAM

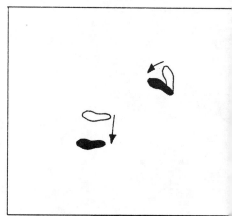

11. MORI JARPKI
(Head Grabbing)

Slide the left foot forward, assuming a left front stance as you extend both hands upward in a grabbing motion.

FINAL FRONT VIEW

TOP VIEW

APPLICATION

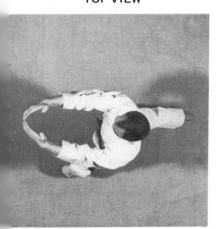

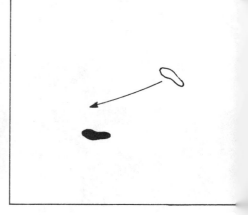

FINAL FRONT VIEW

12. MURUP CHAGI
(Knee Kick)

Pull both hands downward as you execute a middle kick with the right knee.

TOP VIEW	APPLICATION

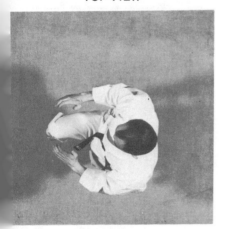

BEGINNING FRONT VIEW

OTHER VIEW

INTERMEDIATE FRONT VIEW

STEP DIAGRAM

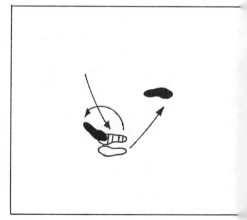

13. SANGDAN YOK SUDO
(High Reverse Knife-Hand)

Lower the right foot to the left foot and then step out with the left foot, pivoting on the right foot 180 degrees counterclockwise. Assume a left front stance as you execute a high strike with the right reverse knife-hand, bringing the left knife-hand under the right elbow joint.

FINAL FRONT VIEW

TOP VIEW

APPLICATION

BEGINNING FRONT VIEW

INTERMEDIATE FRONT VIEW

OTHER VIEW

STEP DIAGRAM

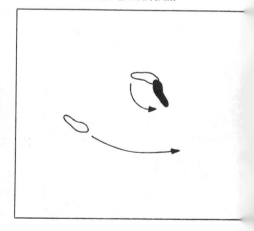

114

FINAL FRONT VIEW

14. SANGDAN TOLYO CHAGI
(High Roundhouse Kick)

Execute a high roundhouse kick with the right foot and then step forward with the kicking foot.

TOP VIEW

APPLICATION

BEGINNING FRONT VIEW

INTERMEDIATE FRONT VIEW

OTHER VIEW

STEP DIAGRAM

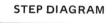

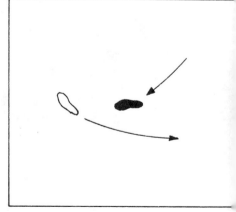

FINAL FRONT VIEW

15. CHUNGDAN DUIRO CHAGI
(Middle Back Thrust Kick)

Execute a middle back thrusting kick with the left foot.

TOP VIEW	APPLICATION

BEGINNING FRONT VIEW

INTERMEDIATE FRONT VIEW

OTHER VIEW

STEP DIAGRAM

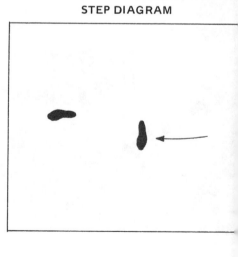

16. CHUNGDAN PALMOK DAEBI MARKI

(Middle Forearm Guarding Block)

Lower the left foot, assuming a left back stance. Then pivot on the left foot 180 degrees clockwise as you execute a middle forearm guarding block.

FINAL FRONT VIEW

TOP VIEW

APPLICATION

BEGINNING FRONT VIEW

INTERMEDIATE FRONT VIEW

OTHER VIEW

STEP DIAGRAM

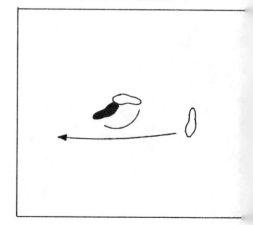

FINAL FRONT VIEW

17. CHUNGDAN TOLYO CHAGI
(Middle Roundhouse Kick)

Execute a middle roundhouse kick with the left foot.

TOP VIEW	APPLICATION

BEGINNING FRONT VIEW   **INTERMEDIATE FRONT VIEW**

OTHER VIEW   **STEP DIAGRAM**

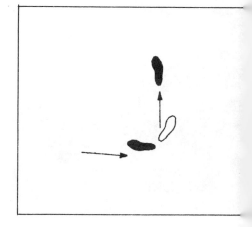

122

18. MONGDOONGEE MARKI

(Stick Block)

Lower the left foot to the right foot. Pivot on the left foot 90 degrees clockwise, then step out with the right foot, assuming a right fixed stance as you execute a stick block.

FINAL FRONT VIEW

TOP VIEW

APPLICATION

BEGINNING FRONT VIEW

INTERMEDIATE FRONT VIEW

OTHER VIEW

STEP DIAGRAM

19. SAM BAEK YOOKSHIP DO TUIYO TOLKI

(360-Degree Jump Turn)

Jump, spinning the body 360 degrees counterclockwise and landing on the same spot, then assume a left back stance as you execute a middle guarding block with the right knife-hand.★

FINAL FRONT VIEW

TOP VIEW

APPLICATION

BEGINNING FRONT VIEW

INTERMEDIATE FRONT VIEW

OTHER VIEW

STEP DIAGRAM

FINAL FRONT VIEW

20. HARDAN KWANSU
(Low Spear-Finger)

Take a straight step with the left foot, assuming a left front stance as you execute a low thrust with the right spear-hand.

TOP VIEW	APPLICATION

BEGINNING FRONT VIEW

INTERMEDIATE FRONT VIEW

OTHER VIEW

STEP DIAGRAM

21. SANGDAN YIKWON TAERIGI HARDAN PALMOK MARKI

(High Back Fist Strike and Low Forearm Block)

Pull the right foot back, assuming a right back stance as you execute a high strike with the right back fist and a low block with the left forearm.

FINAL FRONT VIEW

TOP VIEW

APPLICATION

BEGINNING FRONT VIEW   **INTERMEDIATE FRONT VIEW**

OTHER VIEW   **STEP DIAGRAM**

FINAL FRONT VIEW

22. CHUNGDAN KWANSU
(Middle Spear-Finger)

Take a straight step with the right foot, assuming a right front stance as you execute a vertical spear-finger thrust with the right hand.

TOP VIEW

APPLICATION

BEGINNING FRONT VIEW

INTERMEDIATE FRONT VIEW

OTHER VIEW

STEP DIAGRAM

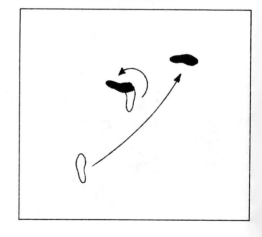

132

FINAL FRONT VIEW

23. SANGDAN DO PALMOK MARKI
(High Double Forearm Block)

Pivot on the right foot 270 degrees counterclockwise, assuming a left front stance as you execute a high double forearm block.

TOP VIEW

APPLICATION

133

BEGINNING FRONT VIEW

INTERMEDIATE FRONT VIEW

TOP VIEWS

STEP DIAGRAM

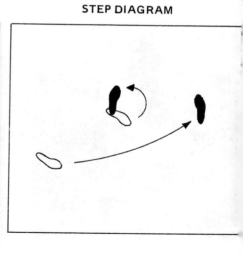

FINAL FRONT VIEW

24. CHUNGDAN PALMOK AP MARKI WA SANGDAN YIKWON TAERIGI
(Middle Forearm Front Block and High Back Fist Strike)

Pivot on the left foot 90 degrees counterclockwise, stepping out with the right foot to assume a riding stance as you execute a middle front block with the right forearm. Then execute a high side strike with the right back fist.

APPLICATIONS

BEGINNING FRONT VIEW

INTERMEDIATE FRONT VIEW

OTHER VIEW

STEP DIAGRAM

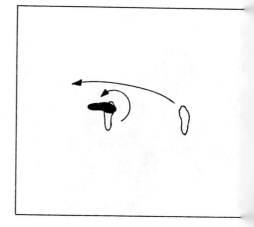

25. CHUNGDAN YOP CHAGI
(Middle Side Thrust Kick)

Pivot on the left foot 180 degrees counterclockwise as you execute a middle side thrusting kick with the right foot.

FINAL FRONT VIEW

TOP VIEW

APPLICATION

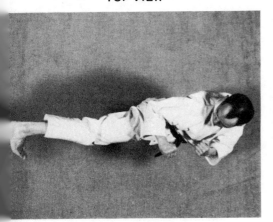

BEGINNING FRONT VIEW

INTERMEDIATE FRONT VIEW

OTHER VIEW

STEP DIAGRAM

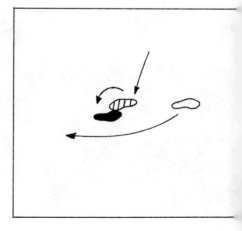

138

26. CHUNGDAN YOP CHAGI
(Middle Side Thrust Kick)

Step out with the right foot, then execute a middle side thrusting kick with the left foot.

FINAL FRONT VIEW

TOP VIEW

APPLICATION

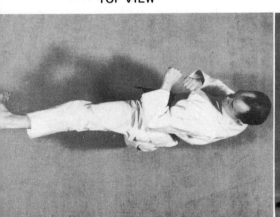

BEGINNING FRONT VIEW

INTERMEDIATE FRONT VIEW

OTHER VIEW

STEP DIAGRAM

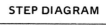

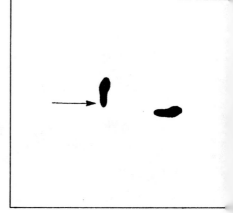

27. CHUNGDAN KYOCHA SUDO MARKI

(Middle X Knife-Hand Block)

Lower the left foot and pivot on it 180 degrees clockwise, assuming a left back stance as you execute a middle X knife-hand block.

FINAL FRONT VIEW

TOP VIEW

APPLICATION

BEGINNING FRONT VIEW   **INTERMEDIATE FRONT VIEW**

OTHER VIEW   **STEP DIAGRAM**

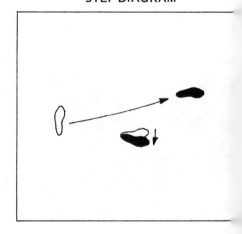

28. DO CHANGKWON WERO MARKI
(Double Palm Fist Block)

Take a straight step with the left foot, assuming a left front stance as you execute an upward block with both palm fists.

FINAL FRONT VIEW

TOP VIEW

APPLICATION

BEGINNING FRONT VIEW

INTERMEDIATE FRONT VIEW

OTHER VIEW

STEP DIAGRAM

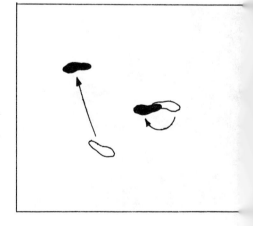

29. CHUKYO MARKI
(Rising Block)

Move the left foot about one-half shoulder's width to the right and pivot on it 180 degrees clockwise, assuming a right front stance as you execute a rising block with the right forearm.

FINAL FRONT VIEW

TOP VIEW	APPLICATION

OTHER VIEW

STEP DIAGRAM

 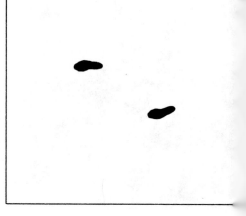

30. CHUNGDAN PANDAE CHIRUGI

(Middle Reverse Punch)

Execute a middle reverse punch with the left fist. ★

FINAL FRONT VIEW

TOP VIEW	APPLICATION

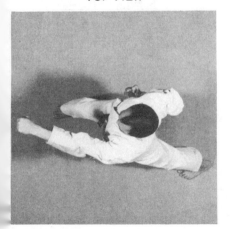

SIDE VIEW

BACK VIEW

OTHER VIEW

STEP DIAGRAM

GOMAN
(End)

Bring the right foot toward the left, assuming a parallel ready stance.

FRONT VIEW

TOP VIEW

APPLICATION

KOREAN COUNTING

1	HANA	1st	ILL
2	DOOL	2nd	YEE
3	SET	3rd	SAM
4	NET	4th	SAH
5	TASUT	5th	OH
6	YAUSUT	6th	YOOK
7	ILGOPE	7th	CHIL
8	YAUDUL	8th	PAL
9	AHOPE	9th	KOO
10	YAUL	10th	SHIB
100	BAIK	100th	BAIK
1,000	CHUN	1,000th	CHUN
10,000	MAHN	10,000th	MAHN